A B C
Animal Alphabet

Brown Watson
ENGLAND
© 2007 Brown Watson, England
Reprinted 2007, 2010

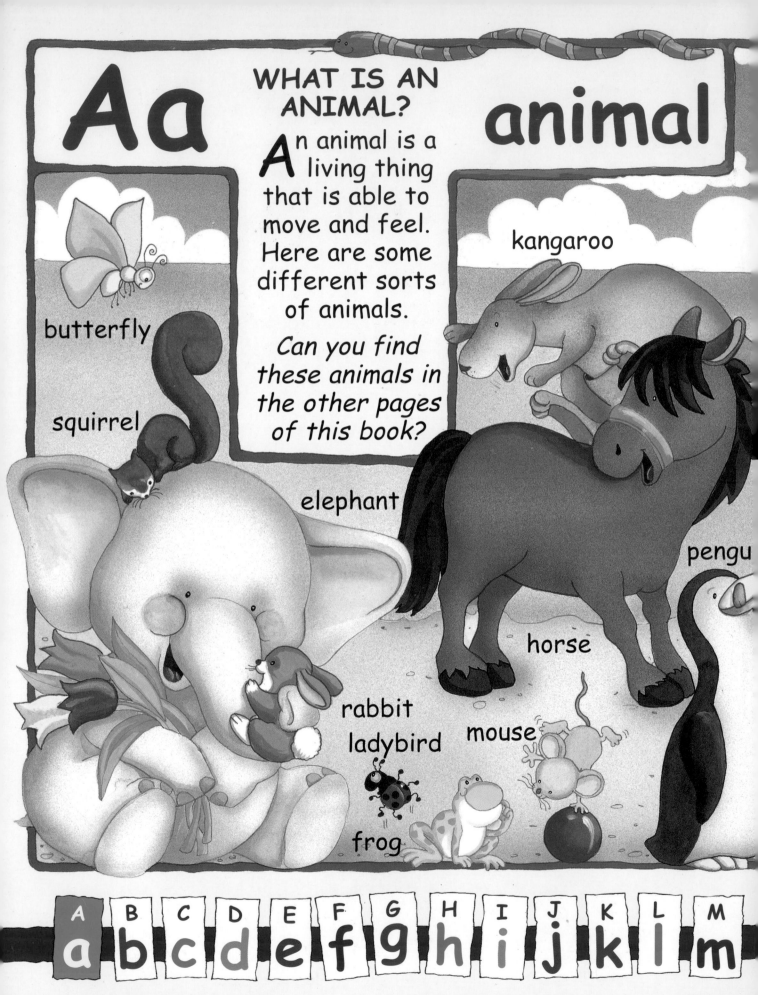

Aa

WHAT IS AN ANIMAL?

An animal is a living thing that is able to move and feel. Here are some different sorts of animals.

Can you find these animals in the other pages of this book?

animal

butterfly

squirrel

kangaroo

elephant

horse

pengu

rabbit

ladybird

mouse

frog

A B C D E F G H I J K L M
a b c d e f g h i j k l m

whale

zebra

giraffe

tortoise

octopus

N O P Q R S T U V W X Y Z

n o p q r s t u v w x y z

Bb butterfly

THE BUTTERFLY'S BEAUTY SLEEP

The beetle's friend was a caterpillar who fell asleep for many years. A shell grew around the caterpillar's body and the beetle thought he would never see his friend again. Then, one day, the shell around the caterpillar cracked and out stepped a beautiful butterfly.

"Yes, it really is me!" the butterfly told the beetle. "Did I never tell you about the magic beauty sleep that turns caterpillars into butterflies?"

Cc

cat

THE CAT WHO VISITED THE QUEEN

A cat went to London to visit the Queen. "Mummy!" cried her baby kittens when she got back home. "Tell us about your day!" Mother cat told how she had frightened away a mouse from beneath the Queen's chair. The Queen was so pleased that she told Mother cat to bring the kittens with her on her next visit. The kittens are now looking forward to meeting the Queen.

N O P Q R S T U V W X Y Z
n o p q r s t u v w x y z

Dd dog

DANNY THE DOG AND HIS BONE

Danny the dog could not find his bone. The rabbit could not help Danny find his bone. The squirrels had not seen his bone. The birds didn't know where to look for Danny's bone. But, the cat was smiling because she had hidden Danny's bone and knew where it was.

Can you see where the cat has hidden Danny's bone?

A B C D E F G H I J K L M
a b c d e f g h i j k l m

Ee  elephant

ELSIE'S SKIP IN THE PARK

Elsie the Elephant's two aunties took her to play in the park. "I wish I'd brought my skipping rope," said Elsie. "Elephants don't need skipping ropes!" laughed Aunt Edna. "We've all got skipping trunks!" laughed Aunt Elizabeth. Then, they held each other's trunks and swung them all around, so that Elsie could skip in the middle of them. What fun she had!

N O P Q R S T U V W X Y Z
n o p q r s t u v w x y z

Ff frog

FROGS THAT CROAK IN THE NIGHT

Three frogs lived in a pond. The big frog croaked: "Croak! Croak!" The middle frog croaked: "Creak! Creak!" and the little frog croaked: "Crick! Crick!" When they all croaked together, they made quite a pleasant chorus. So, every moonlit evening, the three frogs sat on water lily leaves and sang for the king of the goldfish pond and the royal members of his court.

A B C D E F G H I J K L M
a b c d e f g h i j k l m

N O P Q R S T U V W X Y Z

n o p q r s t u v w x y z

Gg giraffe

FOOD FROM THE TOP SHELF

As well as eating grass, many wild animals began feeding on the fruit and leaves of bushes and shrubs. Soon, there was hardly enough food for all of the animal kingdom. So, the giraffe grew its long, long neck to reach high up into the tree-tops for the food other animals could not reach. "Yummie!" said George Giraffe. "The food tastes nice and fresh up here."

A B C D E F G H I J K L M
a b c d e f g h i j k l m

Hh

horse

HARRY'S FAVOURITE DAY

Harry the horse's working life was over and now he lived in a field of his own. Schooldays were his favourite days, because children passing his field would often stop to fuss him or give him a sandwich from their lunchbox. Sometimes they even gave him a lovely red apple!

N O P Q R S T U V W X Y Z
n o p q r s t u v w x y z

Ii

insect

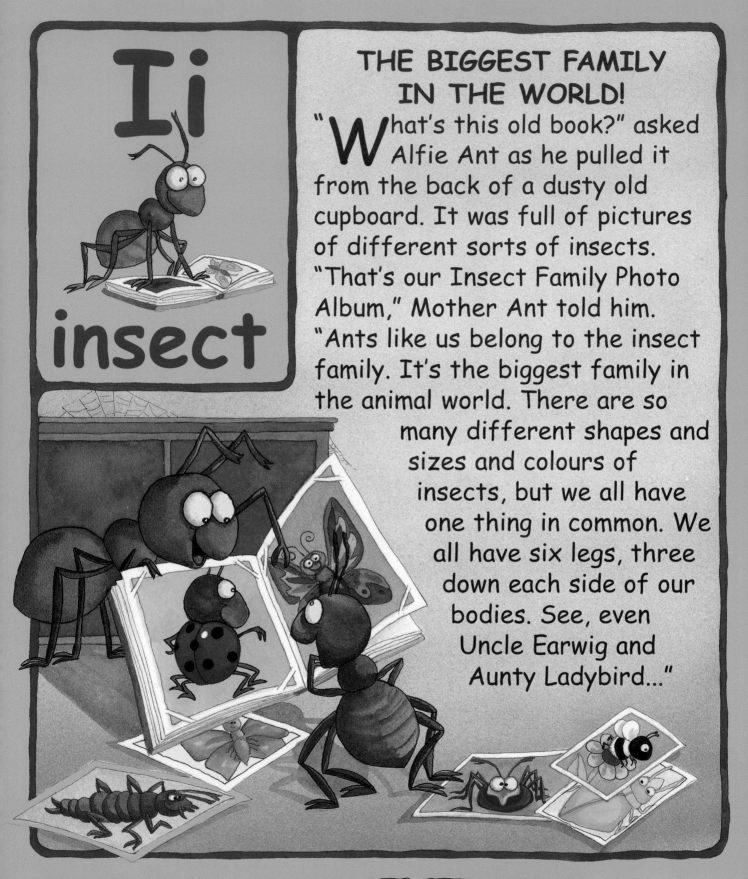

THE BIGGEST FAMILY IN THE WORLD!

"What's this old book?" asked Alfie Ant as he pulled it from the back of a dusty old cupboard. It was full of pictures of different sorts of insects. "That's our Insect Family Photo Album," Mother Ant told him. "Ants like us belong to the insect family. It's the biggest family in the animal world. There are so many different shapes and sizes and colours of insects, but we all have one thing in common. We all have six legs, three down each side of our bodies. See, even Uncle Earwig and Aunty Ladybird..."

A B C D E F G H I J K L M
a b c d e f g h i j k l m

Jj jackdaw

THE FLYING THIEF

The jackdaw birds flew over Katie Kitten. Their greedy eyes looked at the diamond ring Katie's owner had fastened to her collar. It sparkled brightly in the sunlight.

One day, the sparkling ring was missing. "It must have dropped off on the lawn," sobbed Katie. Mother Cat told Katie how jackdaw birds often stole shiny objects. When the jackdaws were away, Katie climbed up the mulberry tree and, sure enough, found the ring tucked away in the corner of their nest!

N O P Q R S T U V W X Y Z
n o p q r s t u v w x y z

Kk kangaroo

KANGAROO'S SPORTS DAY

With the help of big, strong legs and a powerful tail, the kangaroo always won lots of prizes at the Animal Annual Sports Day. With a hop, a skip and a thump of his tail, the bouncy kangaroo took off from the ground. The kangaroo flew high up into the air above the other animals to win the high jump.

A B C D E F G H I J K L M
a b c d e f g h i j k l m

Next, the kangaroo gave another hop, skip and a thump of its tail to win the long jump!

Then finally...

...the kangaroo made lots of little bounces and won the hurdle race!

N O P Q R S T U V W X Y Z

n o p q r s t u v w x y z

Ll ladybird

LADYBIRD AND HER SPOTS

"Ladybirds should be bright red without any ugly black spots," Ladybird told her friend, Beetle. "Just imagine how beautiful I'd look if I was bright red all over." Beetle agreed to paint out Ladybird's black spots. Then, Ladybird suddenly cried: "Ouch!" and jumped back from the peck of a big blackbird.

"Oh, sorry, Ladybird," said the blackbird. "Without your black spots I thought you were a bright red berry, ready for eating."

A B C D E F G H I J K L M
a b c d e f g h i j k l m

Mm  mouse

HAPPY BIRTHDAY MONTY MOUSE

"Happy Birthday, Monty Mouse!" cried Mother Mouse. "Here's your favourite breakfast of muffins with maple syrup." But Monty was too interested in his pile of presents and birthday cards to feel hungry. There was a model plane from Mum and Dad and a computer game from his sister, Mary. Grandma and Grandad had sent him money, because they knew he felt like a grown-up if he went to the shop by himself to choose his own present.

N O P Q R S T U V W X Y Z
n o p q r s t u v w x y z

Nn
nightingale

SWEET SONG OF KINDNESS

The nightingale sings the sweetest song of all birds. Once upon a time, the Emperor of China had a pet nightingale. Each evening he fed the bird in its cage and in return the nightingale sang a song for him. Then, one day, someone left the cage door open and the bird flew away. The Emperor was broken-hearted, but the nightingale returned and told him: "You cared for me very well, so I will return each evening and sing a special song for you."

A B C D E F G H I J K L M
a b c d e f g h i j k l m

Oo octopus

MANY HANDS MAKE LIGHT WORK

"We just don't know how you keep your home so tidy," Mrs. Shark told Mrs. Octopus when all the fish wives met for coffee. "I just can't get home help," moaned Mrs. Cod. "Servants are so hard to find," croaked Mrs. Whiting. Of course, they had all forgotten that Mrs. Octopus had eight long legs, or arms, with suckers to hold things firmly. She was able to dust, wash dishes and do all sorts of other things at the same time!

N O P Q R S T U V W X Y Z
n o p q r s t u v w x y z

Pp
penguin

PENGUIN PARTY

Polly and Peter Penguin were getting ready to go to a party. Pamela Penguin arrived to look after their egg while they were out. She put the penguin egg between her feet to keep it warm. Peter took a long time choosing his tie. Do you think he chose the right one?

They enjoyed the party very much indeed!

A B C D E F G H I J K L M
a b c d e f g h i j k l m

Qq

queen

LONG LIVE THE QUEEN!

There was great rejoicing throughout the Land of the Beehive, where Good Queen Bee ruled over thousands of bees.

The time had come for the Queen and an army of her most faithful workers to leave the hive and fly off to build a new palace in some distant land.

A great feast was held and thousands of bees cried: "Good Luck, Your Majesty!" as the Queen and her workers flew off into the sunshine.

N O P Q R S T U V W X Y Z
n o p q r s t u v w x y z

Rr rabbit

RABBIT'S PUZZLE HOME

The postman told Roger Rabbit that he had so many front doors, he never knew which letter box to pop the letters through. "Oh, any door will do," laughed Roger. "My home is such a mess. I dig out tunnels, or burrows as we call them, and they go this way and that way. Sometimes, I don't know where I am myself."

Can you find your way through Roger's home and out of his back door?

A B C D E F G H I J K L M
a b c d e f g h i j k l m

N O P Q R S T U V W X Y Z

n o p q r s t u v w x y z

Ss squirrel

MOTHER SQUIRREL'S MISSING NUTS

"I'm so hungry, I could eat a whole walnut tree," cried one young squirrel. Mother Squirrel was going to make her family a special nut soup for dinner, but she could not remember where she had put the bags of nuts for safe-keeping.

Can you see where Mother Squirrel put four bags of nuts for safe-keeping?

A B C D E F G H I J K L M

a b c d e f g h i j k l m

Tt tortoise

THE RACING TORTOISE

Some animals laughed at Thomas Tortoise because he moved so slowly. "Well," he told them, "I was the tortoise that once beat a hare in a running race!" After that, the animals treated Thomas very politely. They did not know he was so famous! "I'm not telling them," smiled Thomas to himself, "that during the race the hare was so far ahead he lay down for a rest. I tip-toed past him to the winning post while he was fast asleep!"

N O P Q R S T U V W X Y Z
n o p q r s t u v w x y z

Uu unicorn

THE UNICORN AND THE LION

Long ago, lived an animal called a unicorn. It looked like a beautiful white horse with a long horn growing from its forehead. It was brave and had magical powers and many believed it should be King of the Animals. But, the golden-bearded lion was already King. Three times the unicorn fought the lion for his crown and lost. Finally, because the unicorn had fought so bravely, the lion gave him a golden neckband, decorated with small crowns, and a part of his kingdom to rule over.

A B C D E F G H I J K L M
a b c d e f g h i j k l m

V v

vet

A SPECIAL ANIMAL DOCTOR

Vet is our short name for a veterinary doctor. Vets are special doctors who care for animals when they are hurt, or poorly. This farmer has sent for the vet because his cow is poorly. The vet is giving the cow an injection.

The vet has given some tablets to the sick pig.

The vet has put a bandage over a cut on the dog's leg.

N O P Q R S T U V W X Y Z

n o p q r s t u v w x y z

Ww whale

A WHALE OF A TIME!

Walter Whale floated on the sunlit sea and watched the monkeys in their little boat. "Have you seen Pleasure Island?" the monkeys asked Walter. "We're going there for a picnic". Walter told them Pleasure Island was miles away, but if they liked they could hop up and picnic on his back. That's what the monkeys did. They shared their goodies and lemonade with Walter and they all had a lovely time.

A B C D E F G H I J K L M
a b c d e f g h i j k l m

X x      x-ray

LOOKING INSIDE ANIMALS

When an animal is not well, the vet sometimes takes a special photograph called an X-ray. This helps him to see inside the animal, beneath its fur, feathers or skin. The bones of an animal can be seen clearly on an X-ray photograph.

The vet is looking at the X-ray of a horse.

This is an X-ray of a fish.   This is an X-ray of a bird.

N O P Q R S T U V W X Y Z

n o p q r s t u v w x y z

Yy
young

YOUNG ANIMAL NAMES

Young or baby animals often have special names until they grow up to be like their parents. This young zebra is still with its mother. It is called a foal.

Here are som
and the names o
kangaroo (joey
pig (piglet
cat (kitten
duck (duckling
lion (cub

ther animals
heir young ones...
lephant (calf)
og (puppy)
heep (lamb)
en (chick)
ow (calf)

N O P Q R S T U V W X Y Z
n o p q r s t u v w x y z

Zz  zebra

MOVING TO A NEW ZOO

Zippy was a sad zebra. He lived in a zoo with lots of other animals. They were kept in small cages where people went to look at them. One day, many lorries arrived. The elephants told Zippy they were all being moved to live in a new sort of zoo, which was called a Safari Park.

Life was a lot more fun for Zippy and his friends at the Safari Park.

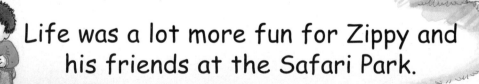

A a B b C c D d E e F f G g H h I i J j K k L l M m

N n O o P p Q q R r S s T t U u V v W w X x Y y Z z